REBIRTH OF THE

VIRGINIA & TRUCKEE R.R.

Amazing Revival of a Steam Railroad

by
TED WURM

 MAY-MURDOCK PUBLICATIONS   ROSS CALIFORNIA

Note: Material in this book has been drawn extensively from
the book SILVER SHORT LINE, Copyright 1983
by Ted Wurm and Harre W. Demoro.

FIRST PRINTING, July 1992

Library of Congress Catalog Card Number 92-13141
International Standard Book Number 0-932916-16-3

Library of Congress Cataloging-in-Publication Data

Wurm, Ted, 1919 -
Rebirth of the Virginia & Truckee R.R. : amazing revival
of a steam railroad / by Ted Wurm.
    p.   cm.
Includes bibliographical references.
ISBN 0-932916-16-3 : $5.95
1. Virginia and Truckee Railroad. 2. Railroads—Nevada.
I. Title.   II Title : Rebirth of the Virginia and Truckee R.R.
TF25.V47W86   1992
385'.09793–dc20

92-13141
CIP

Published by
MAY-MURDOCK PUBLICATIONS
Drawer 1346 - 90 Glenwood Avenue
Ross, CA 94957-1346
for
VIRGINIA & TRUCKEE RAILROAD

Printed in the United States of America

"Probably the most publicized of all short line railroads in the United States is the romantic Virginia & Truckee . . . the glamor girl of all railroads (and) a bright printout of the past when all the world was young . . . the railroad which made possible the Big Bonanza . . . " — *Lucius Beebe, 1947*

Cover photograph: No. 29 above Tunnel 4 en route to Virginia City, 1979 – *Dennis Pisila photo.*

DEDICATION

To the memory of Jim Boynton
who, with his wife, Betty,
founded the Feather River Short Line Railroad
and restored to active service
Steam Locomotive Number Eight.

James E. Boynton
1921 - 1992

Vernon Sappers Collection

H. S. Crocker & Co.'s Print, 42 and 44 J St., Sacramento.

INTRODUCTION

Born in 1869 and destined to become a vital cog in the "Winning of the West," the Virginia & Truckee Railroad (V&T) was built, owned and operated by some of the most powerful men in America. D.O. Mills, William Ralston and William Sharon, through the Bank of California, controlled the major mines and mills of the Comstock Lode. They built the V&T to service their properties. With the crash of the Bank of California in 1875 a new set of "Bonanza Kings" emerged: MacKay, Fair, Flood and O'Brien. The V&T, in addition to its daily chores, worked with Central Pacific to provide in an opulent, first-class service between Virginia City and San Francisco for the movers and shakers of those exciting times.

This great western short line, outfitted with the finest locomotives and passenger cars transporting the potentates of the financial world, operated with a degree of style and grace worthy of its special heritage. And it made money to the extent of being called "The Richest Railroad in the World."

Eventually, with the slowdown of mining and competition from high-ways, business dwindled and profits disappeared. By the 1930s, with 60 years behind it, the once-richest railroad was barely hanging on. In 1938 the line from Virginia to Carson was abandoned. Twelve years later the rest of the tracks, Reno to Minden, were ripped up. Lucius Beebe, who had called V&T "The Golden Railroad to Yesterday," was ready to concede that it was forever. Now that the fires in its engines were cold, he mourned, "it will come not again, for the dead return not."

But the glamor of oldtime railroading as seen in the fire-breathing and whistle-blowing steam locomotive, cannot be driven out of the heart and soul of the west. A far-sighted businessman and railroad enthusiast, Bob Gray, under-stood this and knew that the Virginia & Truckee alone had the history, location and the unchanged scenery to fulfill a longing for oldtime atmosphere as no other rail line could.

The same scenery enjoyed by the nabobs of the nineteenth century was little changed. The basic route to the Comstock was still largely intact and

promised one of the most scenic, most historic, most impressive steam train rides in the Far West. That promise has been fulfilled. Starting in 1968, Bob Gray brought about the amazing resurrection of the old V&T Railroad, and the fascinating story of how he accomplished that is told in word and picture in this book.

Ted Wurm
July 1, 1992

REBIRTH OF THE **VIRGINIA & TRUCKEE R.R.**

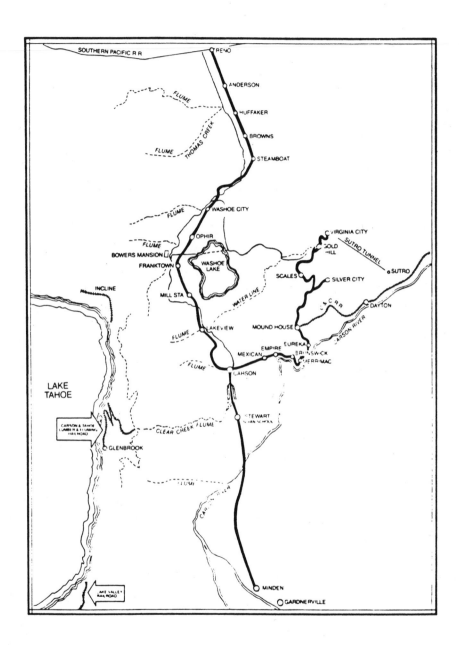

PART I

THE "RICHEST SHORT LINE in the United States" presumably died in 1950. When that unfortunate event occurred, world-renowned *bon vivant* and railroad author Lucius Beebe photographed the last train leaving Carson City, Nevada. Then he walked sadly back to his private railroad car standing near the Carson station and wrote: *"When the Virginia & Truckee banks the fires of its engines at last for the long night, as have so many little railroads before it, it will come not again, for the dead return not."*

Thus died one of the most famous railroads of all time.

Unfortunately — or perhaps it's just as well — Mr. Beebe did not live long enough to be proven a bad prophet. For the Virginia & Truckee (V&T) HAS returned from the dead and crowds of smiling people are happily riding the bright yellow cars, pulled by puffing, whistling steam locomotives, through and around the dramatic mountains of Virginia City's Comstock mines and Gold Hill's spectacular scenery.

In 1975, 26 years after Beebe's prediction of an eternity of sleep for the V&T, and 37 years after the last train whistled away from Virginia City in 1938, tracks were being relaid from the historic buildings of the very place, past the pine nut trees and sagebrush and down the old trackbed. A new enginehouse/shop was being put up where the ancient wooden one had stood for over 80 years.

During the intervening period several efforts were made to restore parts of the railroad, but all failed. Meanwhile, a determined Oakland, California, businessman, Robert C. Gray, did extensive research into county records and approached people who owned lands where the old trains had run. It was a long-time job, full of discouragements. But Bob Gray was driven by a love for the railroad and a determination to see running once again the trains that had fascinated him as a youth.

Gray's present revival of the Virginia & Truckee out of Virginia City has sent a cheering message throughout the West. V&T did not die back in 1950 when last trains were sadly photographed. We like to think it was resting in a well-earned hibernation after 21 active years.

Now we have the yellow cars running again and the tough little steam engines pulling and shoving them around hills and through tunnels. The Nevada scenery has lain in waiting, virtually unchanged in the dry desert air. So today the passengers are able to experience the same breathtaking scenes that the Silver Kings enjoyed back in the 1870s and 80s. Let us go back briefly to those exciting days and see how the railroad came to be and the part it played in the days of the Big Bonanza.

PROSPECTORS APPEARED in what is now the Virginia City area as early as 1852. Surface outcroppings of gold were discovered in 1859 at Gold Hill and in Six-Mile Canyon east of Virginia City. Blue-colored silver ore surrounded the gold rocks and was tossed aside as worthless until assays showed the ore to be worth several thousand dollars per ton in gold and silver. The greatest boom in the history of the West was born.

By 1863 a hundred small quartz mills along the Carson River were grinding the ore that was carried south down Gold Canyon from Virginia and Gold Hill. Important mills gradually came into the hands of Bank of California, represented by William Sharon, as loan payments were missed. The bank's Union Mill & Mining Co. was soon processing most of the ore dug out by miners who had borrowed money from Bank of California.

At the start of 1869 Virginia City, with a population of over 20,000, was among the wealthiest cities in the world and was one of the largest in the West. It was a vibrant and exciting place to be. But during the next few years an economic twilight seemed to be falling upon it.

Among businessmen most aware of this decline was William Sharon, who realized the problem. Transportation of ore from mine to mill by teamsters was so costly that only the richest ores were processed. This cost needed to be lowered to protect the tremendous investment in mines, mills and cities.

Sharon hired mining engineer Isaac James to lay out a railroad from Virginia through Gold Hill and down the mountain slopes to the mills on the Carson River, and thence a few miles westward to Carson City, the state capital. The main line was laid out to start at elevation 6160 feet near the center of Virginia City, two blocks downhill from the business district on C Street and one block down from the red-light cribs on D. About a half mile south was a low ridge to be tunneled; then the surveyed route started its 16-mile plunge toward the canyon of the Carson River. The railroad grade wound around the shoulder of Mt. Davidson, burrowed through two more tunnels and reached Gold Hill station, 6000 feet above sea level. From here a tall wooden trestle was thrown across Crown Point Ravine and the grade dropped downward again along the sides of an ampitheater named American Flat. Five hundred feet of altitude was lost by the time the line left the bowl of American Flat at a tunnel near Silver City. Around the shoulders of hills again the route lost another 500 feet as it reached the mile-long straight stretch at Mound House and the entrance to Carson River Canyon.

Now westward bound, the survey passed eight big mills, some to be served from spurs from the main line and others with their own tramways. Once out of the canyon at Empire, the railroad was free of the river and shot directly westward to Carson City (elevation 4680) at the eastern foot of the Sierra Nevada range. The result was a well-engineered, standard-gauge railroad, 21 miles in length, including a descent of 1600 feet in 13-1/2 miles of heavy construction.

Iron rails from England were brought around Cape Horn. Locomotives were ordered from Booth's Union Iron Works in San Francisco and from Baldwin in Philadelphia, all 2-6-0 type Moguls. Four passenger-train cars were built by Kimball's in San Francisco and four more at V&T's own shops in Virginia City. A first spike of silver was ordered. It was driven into a pine tie at Carson on September 28, 1869, and the entire route was completed on November 12.

On November 29 the first train, pulled by Locomotive No. 1, *Lyon,* reached Gold Hill, followed by No. 2, *Ormsby.* Blasting mill whistles saluted the trains as they rolled along Carson River, through 566-foot American Flat tunnel, over the decorated 350-foot Crown Point Trestle, and pulled among the cheering crowds at Gold Hill. Flags waved, kids shouted, and a cannon BOOMED.

Two months later the first official passenger train reached Virginia City, January 29, 1870. The train pulled up on E Street and triumphantly blasted its deep-toned whistle at the hotels, saloons, and residences perched above, and at the multitude of mine buildings, headframes, smokestacks, and ore dumps below. Cost of the railroad had been $1,750,000 not counting rolling stock and buildings. It was a first class operation in every way, including management.

At the peak of operation some 361 freight cars were in service, plus passenger cars, express and mail cars, and two cabooses. The V&T was carrying more than 40,000 tons of freight per month, almost half of it ore, a third lumber and wood, and 13 to 14 tons of silver bullion from the mills. Having now accomplished its designated purpose of carrying ore down to the mills and wood and lumber back to the mines, it became a logical step to extend the line northward to Reno and a connection with the outside world by way of the new Central Pacific. Construction started at Reno (elevation 4500) in mid-1871. Most of the line was built straight and fairly level for the 31 miles to Carson, surmounting one ridge at Lakeview (elevation 5160), where Tunnel 1 was excavated. Last spike was driven August 24, 1872. Appropriately heading the first Reno-Carson train was brand new locomotive 11, *Reno.*

VIRGINIA AND TRUCKEE RAILROAD.

TIME TABLE NO. 1.

To take effect Monday, July 11, 1870, at 6 o'clock A. M.

For the government and information of Employees only, and is not intended for the public. The Company reserves the right to vary the same as circumstances may require.

	TRAINS GOING EAST.							Distances from Carson	NAMES OF STATIONS.	Distances from Virginia	TRAINS GOING WEST.						
	No. 13	No. 11 Pass.	No. 9	No. 7	No. 5	No. 3 Pass.	No. 1				No. 2	No. 4 Pass.	No. 6	No. 8	No. 10	No. 12 Pass.	No. 14
	P. M.	P. M.	P. M.	M.	A. M.	A. M.	A. M.				A. M.	A. M.	M.	P. M.	P. M.	P. M.	P. M.
	6.00	4.00	2.00	12.00	10.00	8.00	6.00	To	....Carson.... 3¼	21	8.00	10.00	12.00	2.00	4.00	6.00	8.00
	6.17	4.17	2.17	12.17 P.M.	10.17	8.17	6.17	3¼	...Mexican... ¾	17¾	7.45	9.45	11.45	1.45	3.45	5.45	7.45
	6.22	4.22	2.22	12.22	10.22	8.22	6.22	4	...Morgan... 1	17	7.38	9.38	11.38	1.38	3.38	5.38	7.38
	6.28	4.28	2.28	12.28	10.28	8.28	6.28	5	..Brunswick.. 1	16	7.30	9.30	11.30	1.30	3.30	5.30	7.30
	6.33	4.33	2.33	12.33	10.33	8.33	6.33	5½	..Merrimac.. 4½	15½	7.25	9.25	11.25	1.25	3.25	5.25	7.25
	7.00	5.00	3.00	1.00	11.00	9.00	7.00	10	Mound House 2¾	11	7.00	9.00	11.00	1.00	3.00	5.00	7.00
	7.18	5.18	3.18	1.18	11.18	9.18	7.18	12¾	....Silver..... 3¾	8¼	6.45	8.45	10.45	12.45	2.45	4.45	6.45
	7.40	5.40	3.40	1.40	11.40	9.40	7.40	16½	....Scales.... 1	4½	6.25	8.25	10.25	12.25	2.25	4.25	6.25
	7.48	5.48	3.48	1.48	11.48	9.48	7.48	17½	....Baltic..... ½	3½	6.12	8.12	10.12	12.12	2.12	4.12	6.12
	7.52	5.52	3.52	1.52	11.52	9.52	7.52	18	Crown Point 1	3	6.08	8.08	10.08	12.08	2.08	4.08	6.08
	8.00	6.00	4.00	2.00	12.00	10.00	8.00	19	..Gold Hill... 2	2	6.00	8.00	10.00	12.00 A.M.	2.00	4.00	6.00
	8.25	6.15	4.20	2.20	12.20	10.15	8.20	21	...Virginia... To		5.30	7.45	9.30	11.30	1.30	3.45	5.30

READ DOWN ↓   READ UP ↑

MR. H. HUNTER, Train Dispatcher, is authorized to move Trains by Telegraph or otherwise.   ☞ Trains run daily.
Conductor's attention is called to Special Rules governing the movements of Trains by Telegraph.
No Conductor will leave Carson or Gold Hill without ascertaining if there are any orders, and if all Trains due have arrived.
The FULL FACED FIGURES denote meeting and passing places.

H. M. YERINGTON, Supt.

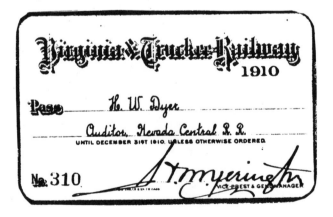

Virginia & Truckee Railway
1910
Pass H. W. Dyer
Auditor, Nevada Central R. R.
UNTIL DECEMBER 31ST 1910, UNLESS OTHERWISE ORDERED.
No. 310
VICE-PREST & GEN'L MANAGER

Switch engine at ore chutes, Ophir Mine, just north of station, Virginia City, circa 1875. *Nevada Historical Society.*

South end, Virginia City, circa 1876. Locomotive 19 or 20, 2-6-0, in foreground bringing in train of loaded wood cars. Mine headframe and tailing piles at right. *Douglas Richter collection.*

Famous V&T enginehouse/shop at Carson City, built 1873. Center is *Tahoe* No. 20; right is *Dayton* No. 18. It was 180 feet across front of eleven massive wooden doors. Demolished 1991. *Daun Bohall collection.*

Morning train crosses Crown Point Trestle approaching station at Gold Hill, 1883. Locomotive *Reno*, No. 11, with cars 13, 14, 3 and 17. Note walkway on this side about eight feet lower than track. Trestle demolished 1935. *Nevada Historical Society.*

Snowy day at Carson City. Plow locomotive No. 18 with Train 2, the *Virgina Express* from Reno. Some winters roads between Carson and Virginia were blocked for up to three weeks. *Al Graves collection.*

Gold Hill about 1905. Virginia City is just beyond "The Divide" (saddle in ridge). Main line above left; spur track below. *Jim Boynton collection.*

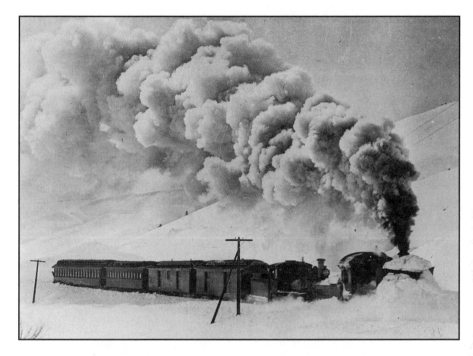

January, 1916. Snow train to Gold Hill and Virginia City, engines 18 and 25. Front windows of 18 covered with boards to protect glass. Jim Savage remembered that snow piled into the cabs through open gangways and covered everything. Soaked through enginemen's clothes until they were wringing wet. *Ted Wurm collection.*

San Francisco Express ready to leave Virginia City shortly before five
o'clock on a summer afternoon in 1905. Engineer Coonie Pohl in cab
and fireman Jim Savage by pilot. At left is long, single-track shed
where passenger cars were stored between trains. *Daun Bohall collection.*

Original Virginia City station here at south end of E Street. Tunnel
(left, with motorcar 99 emerging). Trains of restored Virginia &
Truckee now terminate here, but reopening of E Street trackage would
bring tourist trains closer to town. *Gilbert Kneiss photo.*

Carson enginehouse, July, 1914, showing fronts of locomotives 18, 25, 22, 12; a truly rare coincidence, for all four of these engines have been spared the scrapper's torch. No. 12 (sold in 1938) is at California State Railroad Museum. Nos. 18 (sold in 1938), 22 (sold in 1937) and 25 are featured attractions at Nevada State Railroad Museum, Carson City. *Vernon Sappers collection.*

THE V&T WAS AN unusual little railroad, only 52 miles long in 1880, but tied in with and creating profits for some of the greatest tycoons of the West. It prospered from the start, through good times and bad in the mining business, through the shift to milling in the Virginia City area, through silver strikes, through periods of having more traffic than it could handle. The railroad operated four enginehouses, three machine shops, 24 locomotives, ten passenger cars, and a great assortment of freight cars. It was paying $15,000 in dividends monthly. V&T's primary goal was the transport of freight, so its relatively small number of passenger coaches was not unusual.

Virginia & Truckee produced an offspring in 1880, the narrow-gauge Carson & Colorado Railroad, which headed more or less south from Mound House to reach promising mining claims in the desert toward Death Valley. While the parent V&T had been built to the highest standards of the day, the C&C was only of branch-line standards. This was just as well, because for the first 20 years of its life, the narrow gauge carried little tonnage and few passengers. By 1891, mining booms along the C&C were almost forgotten. The railroad out of Mound House seemed to serve hardly any purpose.

The narrow gauge was sold to Southern Pacific in March 1900 and in May of that year Collis Huntington took a ride over the new acquisition, his train setting a speed record from Mound House to Keeler, 293 miles in 11-1/2 hours. Perhaps he was checking the legendary conclusion of V&T's D.O. Mills: The C&C was built either 300 miles too long or 300 years too soon. The answer came a few months later when the first major silver strike was made at Tonopah. Soon wagon trains were moving ore over 60 miles to the narrow-gauge tracks. Then the Tonopah railroad was built to the junction and thousands of tons of freight moved in both directions at the interchange with V&T at Mound House.

Southern Pacific officials were unhappy over having to remove all freight from narrow-gauge cars and reload onto standard gauge at Mound House. During 1904-05 they converted their narrow gauge, now renamed Nevada & California Railroad, to standard from Mound House to Tonopah Junction and offered to purchase the V&T. But the asking price was too high, so SP in 1905 built a 28-mile line from Fort Churchill on the former C&C to their main line at Hazen, thereupon bypassing the V&T.

Thwarted by Southern Pacific in its attempt to cash in on the

Tonopah bonanza, the V&T still continued to pay dividends primarily because it was the only reliable mode of transportation through semi-wilderness. But as the new century began, Nevada was starting to change. Agriculture nourished by irrigation was becoming successful. So was cattle raising. Under the urging of ranchers and businessmen in Carson Valley, about 15 miles south of Carson City, the V&T on September 10, 1905, broke ground for an extension southward from the capital into the rich agricultural region around Gardnerville. First passenger train ran into the newly-formed town of Minden on August 1, 1906. The main office of the V&T had been moved from Virgina City to Carson in July 1900.

Some mining continued and a few mills in the Comstock area were used in the early years of the Tonopah boom until facilities could be built closer to ore sources. Butters cyanide plant, down Six-Mile Canyon below Virginia City, opened in 1902 and handled much Tonopah material. It closed about 1927. Below Gold Hill, in broad, mountain-enclosed American Flat, where V&T tracks decended on the hillsides, little of any importance had occurred. But in 1920 the United Comstock Mining Company constructed a huge cyanide mill served by a two-mile spur from the railroad. The facility refined low-grade ore and tailings from the area, but this V&T shipper closed in 1926 because of a drop in the price of silver.

Virginia & Truckee Railway (new corporate name since 1904) continued to reflect optimism about the economy of the Reno-Carson area, and the potential of Virginia City mines. Except for the acquisition of three gasoline-powered railcars (McKeen No. 22 and Whites 23 and 99), and purchase of a potential bus competitor, there was little outward change in the going and coming of steam trains. The grand old railroad's activities seemed timeless. With the opening of the Minden Branch, which did bring increased tonnage, three new ten-wheel locomotives were acquired from Baldwin. No. 25 arrived in 1905, 26 in 1907, and 27 in 1913. The latter was destined to be the last engine in revenue service at abandonment in 1950.

Motorcar 23, sometimes called *The Canary*, probably because of yellow brightness and peepy whistle. White motorcar, 1917, at Virginia City on trial run with officials. *White Motor Company collection.*

Motorcar 99 at Virgina City, circa 1927. Supplied to Tonopah & Goldfield Railroad by White Motor Co. in 1921; bought by V&T in 1926. Held Carson-Virginia run five days per week until abandonment of the line in 1938. Yellow body, brass bell. *Arnold Millard collection from Daun Bohall.*

Carson City station and headquarters building July, 1914. Temperature in the 90's. Horse and buggy is stopped on North Carson ("Main") Street. Tracks are on Washington, the main line coming from Reno. The freight depot is building at far right. Note chimneys, protection against very cold winters. *Ted Wurm collection.*

U P INTO THE MID-1920s virtually everything in everyday life along the V&T line arrived by train, with the exception of milk, eggs, hay, grain and meat. But for Prohibition, beer would have been another exception, for Reno, Carson and Virginia had their own breweries. Main newspapers came from Reno, Sacramento and San Francisco. Bread, mail, farm tools and other machinery, repair parts and fuel for autos — most arrived daily on the V&T.

In 1924 the railroad experienced its first year without a profit. Shipments from mining activities had dwindled to practically nothing, but the agricultural branch to Minden had taken up most of the slack. The big railroad shop at Carson was always busy, even soliciting locomotive repair business from other railroads. There was always outside work for the foundry. But growing numbers of autos on constantly improved highways brought a dramatic decrease in railroad patronage. A newspaper story in June 1924 announced the end, after 55 years, of straight passenger trains. Henceforth, all trains (except the "off-peak" motor cars) would be mixed passenger and freight.

A new timetable in September 1932 showed the diminished importance of the Comstock mining area. Trains 1 and 2 would no longer serve the once-mighty Comstock, the Virginia City original line being relegated to branch line status, using rail motor cars most days and a mixed steam train weekly, usually on Saturdays. The Reno trains were shown as now going through to or from Minden and the Railway Post Office cancellation was changed to "Reno & Minden."

It was in 1935 that a mining company did a major relocation for the V&T at Gold Hill, dismantling the landmark Crown Point trestle and replacing it with a deep cut and fill slightly to the west. The miners considered this a small price to pay for being able to get into their rich ground below the old trestle. Arizona Comstock started a big "glory hole" open-cut mine at the south end of C Street in Virginia City, trucking a few blocks to their mill near the railroad tracks. The town's water supply from Sierra Nevada sources had long before eliminated the need for mills on Carson River.

In the middle 1930s mills in Virginia City and at Silver City were rolling, roaring, smoking and smelling 24 hours a day. It was that different smell — pungent, dusty, dry. It may have irritated the occasional tourist come to play the dime, nickel and penny slot machines, but it certainly

didn't bother the natives who relished any job opportunities and could have shouted "WIMBY" (Welcome In My Back Yard). Nor did the growing platoons of railroad enthusiasts mind, for this was part of the color of western mining and desert railroading which had no certain future.

Keeping V&T tracks open in some stormy winters had always been a problem and one locomotive was fitted with a large wedge snowplow on standby in the big roundhouse. Sometimes it took three or four additional engines to help the plow-equipped locomotive charge into massive drifts in Washoe Valley or on the approaches to Virginia City. Train blockades, snowplow derailments and gangs of shovelers were fairly common on the old V&T. On some occasions fuel and provisions ran short and whole communities pitched in to clear the tracks. Southern Pacific sometimes assisted with light locomotives.

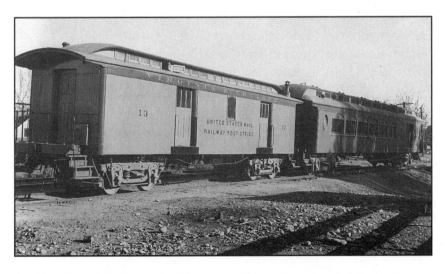

Car 13, originally the bullion car, with reinforced walls, shown here at Reno with combination car 20. *Kneiss photo from Douglas Richter.*

Deserted Brunswick Mill near Empire, 16 miles from Carson City, awaits better times along Carson River, 1916. *Dave Welch photo from Marvin Maynard.*

1924, the last year of straight passenger trains. Here's *Inyo* on Crown Point Trestle at Gold Hill. She left Nevada in 1937 for a fabulous movie career, then was restored at Nevada State RR Museum and went on to stardom at railroad shows in Canada and U.S. Operates periodically at Carson museum. *Nevada Historical Society.*

Gold Hill, June 4, 1938. Engine 11 waits while T&NO boxcar is loaded. The car, larger than No. 11, couldn't be taken to Virginia City because of alleged dangerous conditions in Tunnel 3 which was just out of picture to the right. *Ted Wurm photo.*

Excursion train of Railway & Locomotive Historical Society approaches Gold Hill station from Virginia City July 17, 1938. *Reno* had two flatcars of passengers considered small enough to pass through Tunnel 3 — portal at far right. Firehouse at right still housed a two-wheel hose cart. When building collapsed years later, the wooden tower was mounted on a memorial slab at the site. *Ted Wurm photo.*

OGDEN LIVINGSTON MILLS, grandson of D.O. Mills, was sole owner of the V&T since 1933. He picked up the annual deficits as a sentimental gesture to his family and the booming days of old. Here was the last visible relic and Ogden seemed quite agreeable to keeping it as it had always been. The V&T in the mid-1930s was truly a touch of the past, moving gently through its paces to the delight of the historians and railfans. The sudden death of Mills in 1937 burst the bubble. A year later the V&T was placed in receivership and on March 4, 1938, the Board of Directors passed a sad resolution: "Be it therefore resolved that because of the death of the owner of this railroad, D. Ogden Mills (sic), this road shall cease to operate as a common carrier on a date to be determined."

The original part of the railroad was the first to go. V&T applied for permission to suspend its service between Carson and Virginia City as of May 25, 1938, but Nevada Public Service Commission delayed this by

scheduling a hearing for June 1 in Carson City. At this point, Ward Tunnel (No. 4) between Gold Hill and Virginia City was "discovered" to have alleged dangerous weakness and standard-size freight cars could no longer pass safely through.

An embargo was announced on freight service and a new supplementary timetable issued, effective May 23. It showed no trains between Carson and Virginia for the first time since the line had opened 69 years earlier. There had been a few excursion trains booked, but they would be handled as extras as far as Gold Hill. From the 23rd on, Motor 99 ran as an extra with mail, express, and the occasional passenger. All awaited a decision by Nevada Public Service Commission at the capitol.

On Saturday, June 4, locomotive *Reno* was being cleaned and polished for next day's excursion of California-Nevada Railroad Historical Society of Oakland. Receiver Sam Bigelow got an urgent request to send one boxcar to Gold Hill for loading with sacked ore concentrations. The *Reno* was already under light steam and was sent out extra. She dropped the boxcar at Gold Hill and proceeded through Tunnels 3 and 4, arriving at Virginia City for water and a spin on the turntable. The last carload of freight from the Comstock was taken to Carson and went out on Train 1 late that afternoon. Nevada's PSC granted abandonment permission that day.

Next day, June 5, 1938, was the big Cal-Nevada excursion with nearly 300 passengers in and on seven yellow V&T coaches. Engine 27 brought the train from Reno. *Reno* was added at Carson; passengers were unloaded at Gold Hill and carried into Virginia City by various volunteer drivers of cars, busses, pickups. It was an immense success and brought much-needed attention to the struggling Virginia & Truckee. Various local organizations operated excursions on the trains and there were a couple of additional railfan trips in July by Railway & Locomotive Historical Society. V&T officials began to have second thoughts and shortly thereafter rescinded their complete abandonment plans.

It was 1941 before the railroad finally got around to removing the tracks between Carson and Virginia. They hadn't been used since the 1938 excursions. The rails from Reno to Minden remained in service, since the railroad was now earning a little extra through movie work and the rental and sale of obsolete equipment (engine 12, coach 16, old boxcars, etc.).

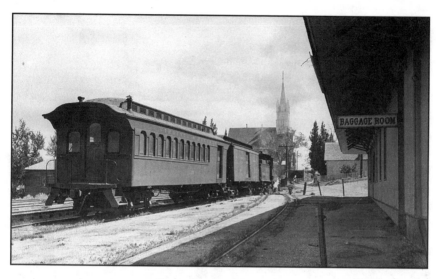

Last scheduled steam passenger train left Virginia City station at 2:25 p.m. Saturday, May 21, 1938. Motorcar 99 carried on until June 3. Here shows the steam consist as it operated in May, 1937. It will pass through E Street tunnel straight ahead (under the street in front of St. Mary's in the Mountains church). Cars 15 and 21. *Gilbert Kneiss photo.*

June 4, 1938. *Reno* gets a drink from double water tank at Virginia City. This day abandonment permission was granted for Virginia City line. Crew: Grover Russell, Harold Brooks, Bill Wise. *Ted Wurm photo.*

Gold Hill in its last train days as seen from *Reno,* No. 11, June 4, 1938, which brought a lone boxcar to be loaded with concentrates. Flanger to left, station, Miners' Union Hall, firehouse. *Ted Wurm photo.*

Excursion at V&T station, Virginia City, July 17, 1938. *Grahame Hardy photo.*

Removing the rails. Three years after the Virginia City line was closed, engine 25 was borrowed by a scrapper in 1941 to remove rails and ties. Income from the sale helped V&T exist for a few more years. *Dave Welch photo.*

Car 11, built by Brill in 1874. V&T's equipment was always well maintained, even when in storage. *Middlebrook photo from Stan Kistler.*

Farewell excursion a year prior to abandonment. Locomotives 27 and 26 en route from Reno stopped at Washoe City for photos. So few passenger cars were left, whatever would still roll, including work cars, was pressed into service. *Bill Pennington photo.*

Train 2, engine 26, crossing Carson River, six miles south of Carson City, in 1950, southbound for Minden in last year of service. Trestle 481 feet across. *Bill Pennington photo from Al Graves.*

Last day of service for Virginia & Truckee. Train 2 from Reno is about halfway to Carson City as locomotive 27, 4-6-0, negotiates Washoe (Allen's) Canyon on May 31, 1950. Fake smokestack was left over from a previous special run. Schedule time was maintained, as usual. *Ted Wurm photo.*

DURING THE WAR years (1941-45) the railroad carried on with only moderate loses, but the first postwar year showed greatly increased expenses which offset increased revenues. *Tahoe*, locomotive No. 20, had been sold for war work; the famous beauty, *Reno*, went to MGM studios in 1945. In October of that same year the extremely competent and well-liked receiver Sam Bigelow died. Management promoted auditor Gordon Sampson to general manager to run the V&T under their strict supervision.

It was downhill all the way. The last of the road's colorful and historic equipment went to film companies. The rare McKeen was sold to become a roadside diner ("too long for our mountain curves," Sampson said). In the late 1940s V&T was operating with equipment that, although worn and creaky, was hardly of the vintage of Comstock history. Sampson could now argue that the V&T worth saving for historical purposes already had been eliminated. In January 1949 the railway applied to the Interstate Commerce Commission and the Public Service Commission of Nevada "for an order authorizing it to abandon...its entire line of railroad extending from Reno to Minden through the counties Washoe, Ormsby and Douglas, State of Nevada."

Both the ICC and the state commission approved the petitions to abandon the Virginia & Truckee. Sampson announced that the last run would be on May 31, 1950. On the fateful day farewell ceremonies were held at Minden (the entire town turned out), at Carson (a subdued ceremony), and at Steamboat Springs, where youngsters sang and a cake was cut. The train arrived in Reno at 6:45, a half-hour late, and was mobbed.

"Hail and farewell to the V&T," editorialized the *Reno Evening Gazette.* "Its homecoming whistle at dusk, sounding across the meadows of Truckee (River) will echo long in the memories of those who knew and loved the railroad."

Although the Virginia & Truckee died as a going concern, it became more important to historians and railroad enthusiasts as its memory faded and those who had seen it passed away. We pointed out at the start that Bob Gray, fascinated with the V&T since boyhood in California, was determined to bring the Comstock portion back to life. Let us see how this almost-hopeless task was accomplished...

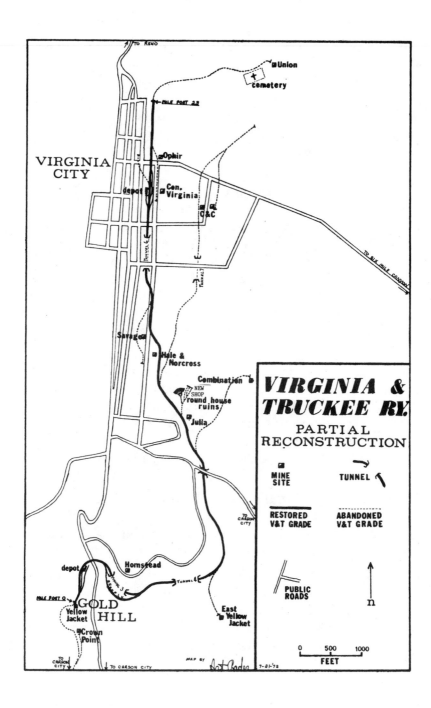

TO RENO

Union

cemetery

MILE POST 23

Ophir

VIRGINIA
CITY

depot   Con.
Virginia

C&C

TO SIX MILE CAÑON

Tunnel 6

Tunnel 7

Savage

Hale &
Norcross

Combination

NEW
SHOP

round house
ruins

Julia

VIRGINIA &
TRUCKEE RY.

PARTIAL
RECONSTRUCTION

MINE
SITE

TUNNEL

RESTORED
V&T GRADE

ABANDONED
V&T GRADE

PUBLIC
ROADS

n

TO
CARSON
CITY

depot   Homstead

Tunnel 3

Tunnel 4

MILE POST 0

GOLD
HILL

Yellow
Jacket

East
Yellow
Jacket

Crown
Point

TO
CARSON
CITY

TO CARSON CITY

MAP BY   Art Caden   7-21-'72

0   500   1000

FEET

PART II

R OBERT C. GRAY, all during his service as a combat photographer in the Marines and his postwar occupation photographing railroad locomotives on a commercial basis, never lost his attraction to the Virginia & Truckee Railway. As proprietor of a book-wholesaling business in Oakland now for many years he had the Nevada short line always in his mind. The V&T of the late 30s was particularly appealing to most Far West railfans. Bob often speaks of the great day when he was one of the 300 excursionists from the San Francisco area who boarded that double-headed (two locomotives) train for the farewell excursion to Virginia City on June 5, 1938.

Gray, as a youthful railroad fan, was thrilled to watch brass-ornamented locomotive *Reno* of 1872 working with the railroad's "youngest" (1913) locomotive No. 27, together pulling the colorful train of clean, well-maintained bright yellow coaches. Most of the cars had been kept in covered storage for 20 years or more. Passengers had to leave the train at Gold Hill because of a weakness allegedly in Tunnel 4 near Virginia City. The engines were allowed to pass through to be turned, but not the passenger cars.

It was a year later that Bob Gray visited the V&T again. He and a fellow railfan followed and photographed locomotive No. 26 with Train 2 (mixed freight and passenger) on its morning run from Reno through Carson to Minden. The friendly, intimate comings and goings, loading

and unloading, switching, fueling, watering provided a vivid contrast to scenes of major railroads near his home in Oakland.

When the Virginia City tracks were gone and only a few crumbling stations remained, when in 1950 the rest of the Virginia & Truckee was thrown on the scrap heap, when strip mining companies began running roughshod over the holy ground of past memories...at this time there could hardly be any doubt that nothing could bring the railroad back to life. During the 1960's tourist railroads were springing up around the country, usually on existing tracks or dormant lines and never, in this country at least, whose tracks had been gone for 20 and more years.

On a business trip to Virginia City in 1965, Bob Gray called on legendary railroadiana collector and dealer Grahame Hardy, who was himself a long-time student of Nevada rail history. Hardy invited Bob to "stay and let's go out for a look at the old right-of-way" near Virginia City. They called on Bob Richards, editor of the *Territorial Enterprise* newspaper, himself a V&T enthusiast. Richards convinced Gray to check county records on the old right-of-way and terminals, all of which appeared amazingly intact and undeveloped.

When surveyor Walter Reed provided right-of-way maps, Gray dropped in at the Storey County courthouse in Virginia City. He met with a certain amount of suspicion. Why would someone from California be interested in an abandoned rail line? They soon came to know Mr. Gray and to accept him, as he kept returning for hours of digging to find out how the parcels of land were laid out and who owned them.

TITLE SEARCH WENT ON over a period of three years, at times needing to check property rights through mixups, non-recordings and other hazards. Easements had to be found and checked. Most of his research had to be done in the assessor's office. In all, there were 68 parcels of land involved, some of the records going back as far as William Sharon and the Bank of California, when original construction of the V&T began in 1868. Some payments recorded were in gold coin. Gray took time out to reincorporate the company in 1972, having purchased title to the Virginia & Truckee Rail*road* (sic) name from Paula, widow of Grahame Hardy. The latter had had the foresight to take over the corporate title upon abandonment in 1950.

Gray discovered in 1965 that key right-of-way property was owned by one man who, needing funds at that particular time, was willing to sell. Bob Gray then appeared one particularly warm evening in the middle of May, 1972, at a special meeting of Storey County Commissioners. They had been called together to hear his appeal for special easments, street-crossing permits, etc. And they were agreeable, but made one condition: he had to start work on the railroad within one year or all would be rescinded.

Property for station area and turntable pit were the key pieces acquired. Then, through easements and purchases, land toward Tunnel 4 was obtained. Other small parcels were picked up through trades. By the beginning of 1975, Bob Gray had all his property together, from the south end of closed Tunnel 6 on E. Street, as far as Gold Hill, a distance of two miles. The original small Virginia City station remains nearby, but the main V&T station north of the tunnel had been dismantled in 1945. The decrepit freight station is still intact. Displayed nearby is locomotive No. 27, a ten-wheel 4-6-0, last engine built for the V&T, in 1913. It's the property of Nevada's governor and, in recent years, a well-maintained engine.

Two blocks uphill, in the main business area, sits car No. 13, which served as V&T's Railway Post Office. Now office of the Chamber of Commerce, the old car has a ticket window at one end for the tourist train and is mainatined by railroad personnel.

The station at Gold Hill survived the years in reasonably intact condition, having been sold on abandonment to Storey County for one dollar. Volunteers from Carson City Railroad Association, starting in 1974, moved in to stabilize the building, install a new roof, and make other repairs to keep the structure sound.

The original trackbed was almost intact, requiring in most areas merely bulldozer work to remove the junk, then clean and level. The highway overpass at south end of town had replaced Tunnel 5 and turned out to be the biggest job in the original restoration. The crew had to resort to blasting, then scaling back the sides of the cut — a strenuous and time-consuming job. A steel two-track shop/enginehouse, 100x40 feet, was erected near the site of the original roundhouse and turntable. Work on this was started early in 1973 and completed in October, thus meeting the

startup deadline. Meanwhile, a search was started for rail and cross ties.

No possible source was overlooked. Western Pacific supplied 1000 ties from an abandoned siding in Feather River Canyon. A tie treatment plant in Alameda, no longer in business, sold all their yard trackage to the V&T — all rails, switches and ties as they lay in asphalt paving. The stuff was in excellent shape. Standard Slag Company offered a nearly-new siding off the Southern Pacific at Wabuska, Nevada. George Squires of Mound House, a long-time friend and supporter of the railroad, went to Wabuska with Bob and was of tremendous help in getting that material to Virginia City. It took many days in the hottest part of September 1973. Standard Oil gave the material from their Reno siding and SP yard tracks at Benicia were bought at scrap price.

Reconstruction started in 1975. A big job was clearing out highway underpass which once was Tunnel 5 at south end of Virginia City. *Bob Gray photo.*

Looking west from highway overpass (former Tunnel 5) as grade leaves
Virginia City for Gold Hill and beyond. *Bob Gray photo.*

Track work progresses southward in area of new shop/roundhouse.
Bob Gray in white shirt checks rails and ties as they line up for highway
underpass. *Virginia & Truckee R.R. Archives.*

Reconstruction scene, F street near station, South end Virginia City. Note Hale & Norcross mine tramway trestle to tailing dump and half buried (right) tank car holding fuel supply. *Bob Gray photo.*

Beyond highway underpass (right distance) track work progresses downgrade toward Tunnel 4 one-half mile beyond. Bob Gray checks with foreman of track gang. *Virginia & Truckee R.R. Archives.*

FIRST RAILS WERE laid and the first spike driven at the shop on May 4, 1974. A pickup truck mounted on rail wheels with tilted steel bed became the "rock truck," distributing ballast as it rolled along. Yard tracks and some of the main line rails were spiked down in 1975. First piece of rolling stock on the restored V&T was Richfield Oil Company tank car ROX905, acquired in good condition at Richmond and trucked to Virginia City to the amusement of town residents. A tank car wasn't exactly what they thought would be rolling into town. Its primary use is for the storage of locomotive fuel.

A small temporary ticket office was opened at the station site on F Street, just south of Washington, in 1975. Three old wooden passenger cars were obtained at this time. Two turned out to have been original coaches 36 and 37 of San Francisco & North Pacific Railroad, a predecessor of the Northwestern Pacific, out of Tiburon. After later service on Southern Pacific of Mexico, the cars were stored at Alameda. Eventually they were "discovered" by Desilu Studios of Hollywood and appeared in many Western movies and videos with such other Desilu stars as locomotive No. 25.

Predictably, the studio found railroad equipment redundant and offered the engine, the three old cars, and other equipment for sale. The State of Nevada badly wanted No. 25 for their proposed museum, but not the other items. An entity called V&T Restoration Company bought some of the rail equipment and sold No. 25 to Nevada. Bob Gray bought the three old wooden coaches. Numbers were assigned continuing the original V&T series, the first being painted yellow and issued No. 25. It was placed on a short section of track near the terminus on F Street to serve as a gift shop, ticket office, and station.

Beside the shop rests Car 26, painted green and awaiting restoration as time allows. The third old coach had served as a work train "dining car" cookhouse on Tonopah & Tidewater Railroad that skirted Death Valley. It is red, numbered 27, and is also awaiting restoration. Cars used in tourist train operation came from Western Pacific, found on a "scrap" siding at Reno — two boxcars and a caboose. Modified, two carry passengers and the third was made into Tunnel Car 54.

In early 1976 an agreement was made with Short Line Enterprises to lease train equipment they also had obtained from Hollywood, a beautiful 4-4-0 steam locomotive of 1881, former Dardanelle &

Russellville Railroad No.8. There were also a caboose and tourist cars, plus a diesel railcar that had been acquired from Tucson, Cornelia & Gila Bend Railroad. It was painted red, given the number 50, and named *Washoe Zephyr.* Much work had to be done on the locomotive because it had been built with a rigid front four-wheel pony truck and couldn't negotiate V&T's sharp curves. So it had to be rebuilt, the first of many major repair jobs done in the V&T shop. The engine was given No. 28 to continue the old V&T number series. The rented Short Line equipment was in service only during 1976, as the rent proved too expensive and Gray preferred to have his own locomotive.

WORD REACHED THE railroad in June 1977 that Willamina & Grande Ronde Railroad in Oregon had a retired steam locomotive for sale. Bob Gray's topped the next highest bidder and two days later he and his crew were at company headquarters in Longview, Washington, to consumate the deal and pick up a shed full of parts at the same time. In the roundhouse at Grande Ronde, Oregon, was No. 680, a 1916 Baldwin 2-8-0. It carried the name Longview, Portland & Northern Ry., another operation of the same firm, but running under the W&GR title when diesels took over. Fortunately, the engine had been stored inside in good condition, but tracks had been cut off just outside the enginehouse. This made removal difficult. Even harder was the task of locating a trucking company to haul the heavy Consolidation to Nevada without being able to use Highway I-5.

Some of the 11,000 pounds overweight was lessened by removing everything that was loose (no cutting). Then they started out, first south on the old highway to Corvallis, thence east over the mountains to Bend and Burns. Turning southerly, the caravan crossed into Nevada at McDermitt and headed for Winnemucca. About 30 miles before they reached the latter, on a Friday afternoon, they had their eighth tire blowout.

The trucker had started out with four spares. Once they were used up, he had been buying more along the way. While replacing the latest flat, Bob was informed that they wouldn't be allowed to drive through Winnemucca on the weekend. However, it was somehow learned that all on-duty police would be having a coffee break at a certain time. That was all Gray needed. He had a half hour to sneak through town.

They made it, and headed west on I-80 (with permit) as far as Lovelock, where they laid over for the weekend. Continuing from there on Alternate 50, they turned off at Mound House and took the heavy load up the mountain via the truck route into Virginia City.

Needless to say, it was a tremendous relief to have that hazardous, stressful journey behind and to have some decent power on hand to pull tourist trains. Gray had been desperate for power early in 1977 and the only available steam engine was a small 0-4-0 Porter saddletank loaned by Erich Thomsen of Redwood Valley Railway. This tiny engine had at one time served as emergency power to help Key System trains off the San Francisco-Oakland Bay Bridge during electric power failures. An air pump was installed at Virginia City and the ''dinky,'' wearing Number 3, was able to perform tourist runs, one car at a time, out of town.

Even with only one car coupled on, the engine had a struggle getting back up the hill and her small water tank had to be filled every other trip. There was a big problem with the 3-Spot's low profile because her smokestack was lower than the roof of an open-side passenger car. While the engine was working, smoke wafted right through, over and among the passengers — steam and whistles and smoke galore!

A tall extension on the stack solved that problem and complete relief arrived when Engine 680 came in from Oregon. She was in such good condition that very little repair work had to be done. After a few trial runs, she was put into service on August 8, 1977, still wearing her LP&N number 680, and just in time to handle a big mob of passengers from a Chrysler Dealers Tour group.

Rebuilding combination car No. 25 to serve as the new station on F Street. Originally it was San Francisco & North Pacific Coast Railroad No. 35 (Northwestern Pacific). *Bob Gray photo.*

Steam train service returns to Virginia City, August, 1976. Locomotive 28, and original V&T caboose No. 10 in bright yellow livery, leased for one year from Short Line Enterprises. Engine readies her train of two gondola cars fitted with passenger seats. *Bob Gray photo.*

Ballast spreading from rock truck on the curve uphill from Tunnel 4 on a hot June 19, 1976. *Ted Wurm photo.*

Revived V&T locomotive 28 (4-4-0) in Virginia City August 4, 1976. Note Virginia City's two famous churches in background, St. Mary's (left) and St. Paul's. *Ted Wurm photo.*

Motorcar 50, *The Washoe Zephyr*, on truck passing restored Fourth Ward School at south end of Virginia City in May, 1976. *Bob Gray photo.*

Chartered freight train approaches Virginia City station November 20, 1976. At end of track the small building is V&T's first station, now a private dwelling. *Robert Dockery photo.*

Tiny 4-wheel steamer No. 3 at uphill (east) portal of Tunnel 4. She started passenger service for 1977 season, couldn't pull many cars and stopped often for water, but held on until mighty No. 29 arrived. *Bob Gray photo.*

No. 680, Longview Portland & Northern Railway (affiliate of W&GR) at Grande Ronde, Oregon, July 1977, ready to load for trip to Virginia City. *Bob Gray photo.*

No. 680 en route. Many stops to replace eight blown-out tires. All obstacles finally overcome. *Bob Gray photo.*

Big No. 29 returns with passengers from Tunnel 4, first run August, 1978, past old Virginia City ruins and ore dumps. Scenery little changed in 100 years. *Bob Gray photo.*

Car 25 completely restored and serving as the new Virginia City station. This old coach was originally SP & NP No. 35, then NWP. *Ted Wurm photo.*

A T THE CLOSE OF 1977's season Bob Gray's V&T had its own locomotive and a sound three-car train. And they had time to get 680 painted and a new number cast. So the attractive 2-8-0 went out of the shop as Virginia & Truckee No. 29 on July 20, 1978. And because she was only three years younger and a member of the same Baldwin Locomotive Works family, 29 fits right in with old V&T 27. Another steam engine was found in 1984, the preserved Southern Pacific switcher No. 1251, product of SP's Sacramento Shops in 1919. The railroad had donated 1251 to the City of Stockton as a monument in a park. City crews had partially embedded the locomotive in concrete, steps on both sides being poured right against the metal. Over the years the engine was surrounded with plantings and two new underground water lines were in the way of removal.

When a previous bidder threw up his hands, the V&T crew laid 350 feet of curving track, supported over the water lines, and dragged 1251 out. They crossed the Sierra Nevada mountain range by way of 8600-foot Kit Carson Pass and delivered the locomotive to Virginia City early in July, 1984. To the accompaniment of many toasts and sighs of relief, the engine was unloaded from her nine-axle trailer and placed on V&T rails. Examination showed the boiler to be in good condition, in spite of 30 years in the park. Work on restoration of 1251 is scheduled to start in summer, 1992, in the railroad's well-equipped shop, under the supervision of a entirely capable full-time machinist.

Another operating steam locomotive arrived for the 1991 season. It is Feather River Short Line No. 8, a 1907 Baldwin 2-6-2 which originally worked on Hobart Southern Railroad out of Truckee. Restored at Quincy and Portola by owners Jim and Betty Boynton, the 8-spot was looking for a place to operate and met up with Bob Gray at the right moment. Jim (to whom this book is dedicated) was a retired Western Pacific engineer and the two men had been friends since the 1930s. No. 8 is a fine engine, looking and sounding perfect for the Comstock Lode environment and contributes to a breathtaking sight when doubleheaded upgrade out of Gold Hill with No. 29.

A LITTLE MORE THAN a mile from Virginia City station, on a descending grade, is East Yellow Jacket Tunnel No. 4. This 401-foot bore was in fairly good condition when restoration began. Track crews were able to do most of the cleaning with a bulldozer. After the upper portal was rebuilt, the tourist train locomotive could back part way in for photos when running around the train. Tunnel car 54 was used during the installation of steel sets (braces) to hold back the sides and ceiling. They used new sets purchased by SP for a Northwestern Pacific tunnel, but not used. Tom Gray, Bob's son who worked strenuously for several years as superintendent of the railroad, welded all sets as they were installed, ten feet apart. At the lower portal toward Gold Hill there was much difficult repair work, requiring steel sets only five feet apart.

Tunnel 4 was finally opened all the way in June 1987. Then they tackled Tunnel 3, almost in Gold Hill. This was actually the tunnel that allegedly showed weakening back in 1938, giving the railroad an excuse for immediate abandonment. It was 250 feet long, and except for portals, appeared to be in good condition. Several mining engineers were consulted and there was some doubt as to the overhead stability. It was decided to take a calculated risk and and try to avoid the consequences of having to build a line around the hill. Gray's crew had started placing sets when a massive overhead boulder loosened and slowly settled while workmen were away. All material in the restored area was crushed.

Then the only way to reach Gold Hill station was to construct a huge fill around the end of this ridge and place the tracks out as far as possible without making a curve too sharp for steam locomotives. Forty thousand yards of material were required, much of it being debris from the tunnel collapse and the balance excavated from the hill itself. So now, instead of going through the hill, trains run around it on a 19-degree curve which opens a spectacular view to hundreds of square miles of Nevada scenery to the south and west. Work on the tunnel will still continue on an indefinite basis so that eventually it can be used for downward trains, leaving the scenic outlook for those climbing the steep grade.

Tracks reached the major goal, old Gold Hill station, in June 1991, crossing steep old-route Highway 342 at a sharp curve just below Tunnel 3. The red station is still intact, saved by Storey County ownership and some very dedicated volunteers. A new group from Virginia City, the Comstock Historical Restoration Foundation, took over restoration,

including a train ticket office and other amenities. Former "ghost town" buildings that stood near the station (the tracks curved between them) were Miner's Union Hall and the two-story firehouse. Both gradually collapsed into ruins over the years, leaving only the firehouse steeple placed as a monument.

Gold Hill station sat deserted in May, 1980, (but not forgotten) for over half a century (1938-1992), threatened by mining company encroachments from south and west. *Ted Wurm photo.*

May 31, 1980. Old V&T railway post office car 13 sits opposite the post office and next to old firehouse/museum and serves as uptown ticket office for train rides. *Ted Wurm photo*.

1983 — preparing east (uphill) portal Tunnel 4 prior to installation of steel sets. *Bob Gray photo.*

Tunnel 4 bracing — steel sets spaced 5 feet apart at portals, 10 feet through solid interior. Tom Gray, Bob's son, welding. Younger Gray maintained and ran motive power during first years of operation. *Bob Gray photo.*

Ex-SP 0-6-0 switcher 1251 at Stockton Park, June, 1984, following nearly 30 years of clambering kids. *Bob Gray photo.*

Pulling 1251 out of Stockton park, July 1984. *Bob Gray photo.*

V&T No. 29 pulls 1251 off highway trailer at Virginia City, July 1984.
Note gondola car used as "idler" to distribute weight on temporary rails.
Bob Gray photo.

June 5, 1938. (above)
"Farewell" excursion train of
1938 approaches Virginia City.
Locomotives *Reno* No. 11 and
No. 27. Both survive today: *Reno*
is in film work, 27 displayed at
Virginia City (as this is written).
June 5, 1991, (right) Same scene, same grade. Note pine nut trees have
grown but little else has changed in the dry Nevada air. Locomotives
are V&T 29 and Feather River Short Line 8 headed back to the tourist
railroad enginehouse. *Ted Wurm photo.*

Special "farewell" passenger train stops at Gold Hill station June 5, 1938. Entering the bus for Virginia City (left) passengers include Bob Gray (seen through door window) who would bring the V&T railroad back to this spot exactly 53 years later — June 5, 1991. *Ted Wurm photo.*

The second double-header exactly 53 years after the "farewell" train of June 5, 1938, is given special permission here to use the new crossing before completion. Some of the original excursionists were there to watch and ride. The station is undergoing restoration. *Ted Wurm photo.*

Across the tracks at the new Gold Hill crossing is a monument, the cupola saved from the collapsed firehouse. Great background sight and sound as doublehead "memorial" train climbs 4% grade back to Virginia City, both engines (V&T 29 & FRSL 8) working hard. *Ted Wurm Photo.*

Feather River Short Line No. 8 (Baldwin 2-6-2, 1907) offloading at F Street, Virginia City, on a cold October 19. 1990. *J.E. Boynton photo*.

Feather River Short Line No. 8, Virginia City, June 5, 1991. *Ted Wurm photo.*

Sturdy Oregon lumber hauler No. 29 (2-8-0) made herself right at home among mine ruins and excitements of the great Comstock mine area. She is truly "Queen of the Comstock" in her new paint. *Bob Gray photo.*

JUST A HUNDRED yards or so beyond the station once stood the famed Crown Point Trestle that carried tracks over a steep ravine. A mining company got permission in 1935 to demolish this and dig out the rich ore below. They replaced it with a monstrous fill, using material from the big cut they had to excavate beyond for trains to pass. Recently, farther along, there had been much destructive open-pit mining which has left deep Overman Pit where V&T trains used to begin their descent toward Mound House and the Carson River gorge. When V&T is ready to lay tracks beyond Gold Hill, Bob Gray is confident this area will not be a major obstacle, hardly up to some of the others he has already overcome.

Running Virginia and Truckee trains beyond Gold Hill? It is within the realm of possibility that the original 1869 grade will be opened around the bow-like sides of American Flat, past or through damaged Tunnel 2, to the spacious area at Mound House. There is even speculation about getting tourist trains back through the canyon above Carson River as far as Empire, only a few miles from Carson City. It seems to make sense for casinos and other businesses in the State Capital to have such a proven tourist attraction almost at the doorstep.

Another move being discussed for the restored Virginia & Truckee is to extend track northward from the terminus at Virginia City. Rails could be placed back where the E Street Tunnel (now filled in) was, in front of the Church of St. Mary's in the Mountains. This would take the trains closer to the main part of town and right at the location of the main V&T station that was removed after abandonment. Businessmen have noted that the railroad carried 62,000 passengers in 1991, up 25% in just three years, and they would welcome this accessibility.

To visitors, collectors and railroad fans looking for a link to steam trains and the Bonanza Days on the Comstock, here is the real thing. The V&T train ride of today is truly unique. Started in 1976 on a trackbed over 100 years old and departing from still-fabulous Virginia City, it has all the atmosphere of world-famous Comstock Lode's gold-mining and silver-booming Big Bonanza. Steam train whistles add authenticity to the scene.

Visual evidence and relics of mining days are everywhere and the train passes most of them. Up on a hillside to the right is the restored mansion of John W. Mackay, founder of Mackay Wireless and widely acclaimed as "Richest Man in the World." Beyond is marvelous four-

story Fourth Ward School. It was falling into ruin 40 years ago, but now is one of the great beauties of the past.

Tracks lead us through mine ruins, under overhead tramway trestles, past ore dumps and mill tailings. We pass the modern shop/roundhouse where all rail equipment is restored and maintained. Next comes a highway overpass, once Tunnel 5, and then we start downgrade passing many ancient pine nut trees that were growing here when the first V&T trains whistled past with strings of richly-loaded ore cars en route to be processed in mills then strung along Carson River below. Soon we are entering Tunnel 4 through which tracks were restored as recently as 1987.

Out into daylight again, almost surrounded by rocky hills producing the pungent smell of sagebrush. Ahead lies Tunnel 3, which collapsed during restoration efforts in 1989 (no one hurt). It is now cleared out and will have tracks running through in a few years. Meanwhile, the train swings left and continues along the edge of the big fill built to carry tracks around the tunnel. Ahead and to the left is one of the most thrilling views of oldtime Nevada landscape.

Descending around the curve, we arrive in the near-ghost town of Gold Hill. The train crosses a minor highway here over the latest high-tech, government-specification railroad crossing. It works fine, but certainly doesn't add to the oldtime atmosphere. Here we are at aged red station, preserved over the years since the last train left in 1938, more than a half century ago. Down the road a short distance can be seen historic Gold Hill Hotel, a fine brick building that survived through the 1960s as a three-woman bordello. There is an antique bar in this old structure, while a modern restaurant and hotel has been tastefully added at the rear. Other buildings survive around the townsite.

When the conductor shouts "ALL ABOARD" for the return climb to Virginia City, the heavy exhausts of the smokestack signify a real struggle up the steep grade. Think how it must have been 120 years ago as up to 45 trains each day followed this very route with some of the richest cargo ever hauled and several of the world's richest men.

You will be riding the last remaining segment of the famous "Silver Railroad to Gold Hill," sprung back to life through determination, hard work, and lasting affection for the past. Reviving of the Virginia & Truckee Railroad and bringing it back to the city of its birth

has sent a heart-warming message to western historians and railroad fans. The V&T did not die back in 1950. It was hibernating and it has now been awakened through the efforts of alert and dedicated people.

SURVIVING LOCOMOTIVES OF ORIGINAL V&T RAILWAY

Number/Name	Type	Built	Disposition
11 *Reno*	4-4-0	Baldwin 1872	Film work in Arizona
12 *Genoa*	4-4-0	Baldwin 1872	CA State R.R. Museum
13 *Empire*	2-6-0	Baldwin 1872	C.S.R.M. (Original No.15)
18 *Dayton*	4-4-0	SP Shops 1873	NV State R.R. Museum
20 *Tahoe*	2-6-0	Baldwin 1875	PA Historical Museum
21 *JW Bowker*	2-4-0	Baldwin 1875	CA State R.R. Museum
22 *Inyo*	4-4-0	Baldwin 1875	NV State R.R. Museum
25 —	4-6-0	Baldwin 1905	NV State R.R. Museum
27 —	4-6-0	Baldwin 1913	Displayed at Virginia City

NOTE: Out of 29 owned locomotives, NINE survive
and seven of these are over 115 years old.

CHRONOLOGY

PART I

1868   March 5 — Virginia & Truckee Railroad incorporated.

1869   February 18 — Construction started on V&T R.R. at Virginia City.

        November 29 — First passenger train, Carson City to Gold Hill.

1870   January 29 — First passenger train steams into Virginia City.

1872   August 24 — Extension to Reno opened, completing the railroad from Virginia City to Truckee River.

1873   July 4 — Massive stone enginehouse/shop opened at Carson City, 322x180 feet, eleven tracks into front doors. (Demolished 1991.)

1880   May 10 — Subsidiary Carson & Colorado Railroad incorporated. (Sold to SP in 1900.)

1900   July 12 — Railroad offices moved from Virginia City to Carson City.

1904   July 4 — Reincorporated as Virginia & Truckee Railway. (Note change of name.)

1906   August 1 — First passenger train on new branch to Minden.

1924   August 1 — Corporation declares last dividend.

1937   August 1 — Owner and president Ogden L. Mills dies.

1938   June 4 — Nevada Public Service Commission grants permission to abandon line from Carson to Virgina City.

        June 5 — Farewell excursion to Virgina City.

1950   May 31 — Remaining line, Reno to Minden, abandoned.

PART II

1965   May 31 — Robert C. Gray visits Virginia City on business and notes right-of-way intact.

1972   May 31 — Storey County Commissioners approve. Rail line out of Virginia City incorporated as V&T Rail*road*. (Note change of name *again*.)

1974   May 4 — First rails laid for Virginia & Truckee revival.

1976   July 2 — First revenue train on reborn V&T R.R.

1977   June — Locomotive 29 acquired from Oregon (Ex-Longview Portland & Northern Railway No. 680).

      July 19 — Locomotive 29 makes her debut, first passenger run.

1980   May 31 — State opens V&T Museum at Carson City.

1987   July 10 — Tunnel 4 officially opened.

1989   October 19 — Feather River Short Line No. 8 comes to work on V&T.

1991   June 5 — No. 29 and No. 8 doublehead to open line back to Gold Hill. (53rd anniversary of "last train").

SUGGESTED FURTHER READING

Silver Short Line by Ted Wurm & Harre Demoro — a complete illustrated history of Virginia & Truckee and it environment, re-published by V&T in 1988.

Beebe, Lucius & Clegg, *Virginia & Truckee*, Oakland, G. Hardy, 1949.

Beebe & Clegg, *Legends of the Comstock Lode*, Oakland, G. Hardy, 1951.

Beebe & Clegg, *Steamcars of the Comstock*, Berkeley, Howell-North, 1957.

De Quille, Dan, *The Big Bonanza*, New York, Knopf, 1947.

Ferrell, Mallory H., *Slim Princess*, Edmonds, Pacific Fast Mail, 1982 (C&C).

Glasscock, C.B. *Big Bonanza*, Indianapolis, Bobbs-Merrill, 1931.

Kneiss, Gilbert, *Bonanza Railroads*, Stanford University Press, 1941.

Koenig, Karl, *Virginia & Truckee Locomotives*, Burlingame, Chatham, 1980.

Lord, Eliot, *Comstock Mining & Mines*, Berkeley, Howell-North, 1959.

Stewart, Robert & M.F., *Adolph Sutro*, Berkeley, Howell-North, 1962.

FIRST TRIP OF LOCOMOTIVE NO. 29

ALL LOCAL RESIDENTS ARE INVITED TO BE OUR GUESTS ON WEDNESDAY NIGHT July 19th 1977 at 7:00 P.M. to help us celebrate the inaugural service of locomotive number 29.

Entertainment will be provided on the train. The train will depart from the V&T station near Washington & 'F' Streets.

On Thursday morning July 20th we will commemorate the first scheduled revenue trip of number 29 at 10:30 A.M. by carrying a sack of specially prepared mail for the occasion. This is the first mail carried on the V&T since the last trip in 1950. The stamps used will be ones issued over 25 years ago showing historic railroad events. A picture of number 29 is on the envelope and these will be cancelled on that date.

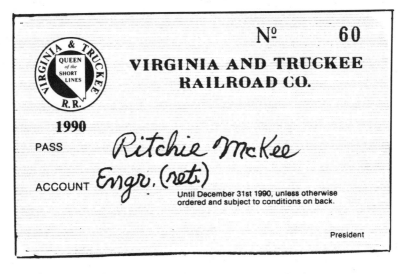

Nº   60

VIRGINIA AND TRUCKEE RAILROAD CO.

QUEEN of the SHORT LINES

VIRGINIA & TRUCKEE R.R.

1990

PASS   *Ritchie McKee*

ACCOUNT *Engr. (ret.)*

Until December 31st 1990, unless otherwise ordered and subject to conditions on back.

President

ACKNOWLEDGEMENTS

Special thanks to the authors of *Silver Short Line,* the definitive history of the Virginia & Truckee Railroad. Copyrighted permission provided that this guide would furnish modern-day V&T visitors with some idea of how it all came about, how its bright flame was extinguished, and how its remarkable revival was accomplished.

The author and publisher are indebted to the following persons and institutions from whom photographs were borrowed: Daun Bohall, Betty and James* Boynton, Robert Dockery, Robert Gray, Gilbert Kneiss,* Nevada Historical Society, William Pennington,* Douglas Richter, Vernon Sappers, University of Nevada Library, David Welch,* Walter Young.*
* - deceased

Dick and Jayne Murdock of May-Murdock Publications have the author's sincere thanks for advice and for their expertise in the design and layout of this book.

COLOPHON

Typesetting: R. Nolan & Sons, 4460 Redwood Hwy, San Rafael, CA using MagnaType on IBM PCs translated with Blueberry Software, Qume laser proofs, final output Agfa 8400.

Typeface: Bem

Photostats: Fast Stats/Type & Graphics, 1215 Second Street, San Rafael, CA

Printing & binding: Thomson-Shore Inc., 7300 West Joy Road, Dexter, MI

Paper: 60# Glatfelter Thor white, acid-free recycled

Ink: soy based

Color separation: Image Arts, 919 Filley Street, Lansing, MI

TIME TABLE

Thrill to the Sights and Sounds
of Historic
Steam Locomotives

FARES
(All round-trips)

Adults	$3.25
Children	$1.50
All day pass	$6.00

Special excursion and party trains available.
Phone (702) 847-0380

DISTANCE BY HIGHWAY TO VIRGINIA CITY

Reno to Virginia City 21 mi.
Carson City to Virginia City 14 mi.
Lake Tahoe to Virginia City 27 mi.
Sacramento to Virginia City (via Reno) 145 mi.
Sacramento to Virginia City (via Carson) 147 mi.
San Francisco to Sacramento 80 mi.

SCHEDULES
1989

Trains will operate roundtrip everyday
from May 27th through October 1st.

Train No.	Depart Virginia City	Arrive Virginia City
1	10:30 AM	11:00 AM
2	11:15 AM	11:45 AM
3	12:30 PM	1:00 PM
4	1:15 PM	1:45 PM
5	2:00 PM	2:30 PM
6	2:45 PM	3:15 PM
7	3:30 PM	4:00 PM
8	4:15 PM	4:45 PM
9	5:00 PM	5:30 PM
10	5:45 PM	6:15 PM

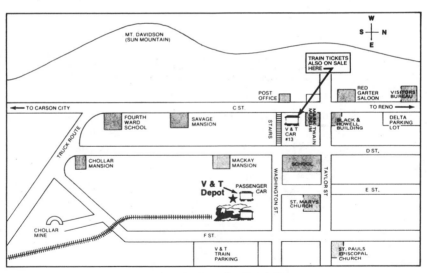

Turn downhill at Taylor St. in Virginia City

VIRGINIA CITY
HISTORIC TRIO TOUR

UNUSED PORTIONS OF THIS TICKET NON-REFUNDABLE

CHOLLAR MINE	MACKAY MANSION	VIRGINIA & TRUCKEE RAILROAD

CHOLLAR MINE	MACKAY MANSION	VIRGINIA & TRUCKEE RAILROAD	№ 7

Conductor's Stub

№ 003

WASHOE ZEPHYR

QUEEN *of the* SHORT ROUND TRIP PASSAGE

Between Virginia City and Tunnel No. 4

Goldhill, Nevada

№   003

ADULT

O116

ADMIT ONE TO:

THE GRAND OPENING OF
THE VIRGINIA & TRUCKEE R.R.
TUNNEL #4

FRIDAY, JULY 10, 1987   7:00 P.M.

(Beginning promptly with train ride)
Buffet Dinner Included

Park at the Gold Hill Hotel or
the V&T R.R. parking lot
(Shuttle between two provided)

847-0111   *847-0380*

Additional copies of this book available through
Virginia & Truckee R.R.
P.O. Box 467
Virginia City, NV 89440
Phone: (702) 847-0380